LOST IN CYBERSPACE

Alan Richter
Carol Willett

JOSSEY-BASS/PFEIFFER
A Wiley Company
www.pfeiffer.com

Published by

JOSSEY-BASS/PFEIFFER

A Wiley Company
989 Market Street
San Francisco, CA 94103-1741
415.433.1740; Fax 415.433.0499
800.274.4434; Fax 800.569.0443

www.pfeiffer.com

Jossey-Bass/Pfeiffer is a registered trademark of Jossey-Bass Inc., A Wiley Company.

ISBN: 978-0-7879-5985-2

We at Jossey-Bass strive to use the most environmentally sensitive paper stocks available to us. Our publications are printed on acid-free recycled stock whenever possible, and our paper always meets or exceeds minimum GPO and EPA requirements.

Acquiring Editor: Josh Blatter
Director of Development: Kathleen Dolan Davies
Editor: Rebecca Taff
Senior Production Editor: Dawn Kilgore
Manufacturing Supervisor: Becky Carreño
Cover Design: Chris Wallace

CONTENTS

LOST IN CYBERSPACE

INTRODUCTION

Good heavens! Your boss has given you just seventy-two hours to pull together a globally dispersed team to create a web-based presentation on collaborative best practices for the client of a lifetime. What do you need? Who do you need? What do you do first? Time is running out! *Lost in Cyberspace* challenges you to develop your consensus building and group decision-making skills within tight deadlines against the high expectations of a demanding client.

Your task will be two-fold:

- To review The Scenario, then individually select and rank the ten *most critical* items from a list of tools and resources that will enable you to meet CyberSpec's expectations.

- To develop a group consensus about what it will take for you to succeed in accomplishing your mission and, on that basis, develop a group ranking of the available resources.

THE SCENARIO

It's Monday at 4:59 p.m. Eastern time when the phone rings. The minute you answer the telephone your manager snaps in a tense voice, "Is that you?" Before you can respond, she quickly continues, "Look, we've got a 60 percent probability to close on the e-commerce deal of a lifetime if we can put together a winning presentation on our virtual team skills and deliver it by Friday at 1:00 p.m. in Wagga Wagga—you know, Wagga Wagga, Australia?—I think they're fourteen hours ahead of us.

"CyberSpec, Inc. is giving us a chance to become their sole solution provider and strategic alliance partner in our market if . . ." the voice on the line becomes ominous, "*if* we can prove our mastery of web-based collaboration techniques by pulling together a globally dispersed design team to make a winning online capabilities presentation to them on Friday. This could be worth millions and a commanding position in the market if we can beat the competition. CyberSpec is only interested in partnering with organizations that can meet their requirements of cyber-collaborative sophistication. Traditional, geographically limited, face-to-face teams need not apply.

"You don't have much time to identify the people you need, to organize the technical tools, and to determine how you're going to collaborate as a team to create this presentation. With time zone differences, you have only about seventy-two hours to complete the task. You must establish a web-based global team that can work virtually and deliver a winning online presentation that highlights our collaborative skills. We must show that we not only know the tools but also that we know how to use them to work with anyone, anywhere, anytime."

As you try to control your panic, your manager goes on to list the proposal specifications. "They say we must:

- Create a geographically and organizationally diverse team without face-to-face contact;

- Identify, use, and effectively integrate the knowledge of all team members;

- Show our mastery of synchronous and asynchronous collaborative tools; and

- Demonstrate how fast we can respond to this e-commerce opportunity.

"And also," she draws a deep breath, "it says here we need to make our presentation virtually to the CyberSpec people. They're not just looking for a document attached to an e-mail or some boring PowerPoint slides. They want to see how effectively we can facilitate an interactive online conference without booking airplane tickets. Good thing you went to Wharton, huh? Do you have any questions?"

She was off the line before you could say, "Well, as a matter of fact I do."

As you slowly hang up the phone, it occurs to you that this is more than just a technology problem. This is a people problem, an information problem, and a team-building problem. To solve it requires some thoughtful choices among a range of communication tools, information resources, and team skills. You have very little time in which to act. If you are to succeed in assembling your virtual team and producing the winning presentation for CyberSpec, Inc., you must choose wisely.

YOUR TASK

Do not communicate with anyone else for this portion of the activity. Your individual task is to select and rank ten resources in total from the list of tools, information, and team expertise on the following pages. (Refer to the Glossary of Terms on page 6 if you have questions about items on the list.) First, place a check mark in the "Selections" column next to each of the ten items you believe is most critical to your virtual team's success. You will have ten minutes to select your top ten items.

After completing your selections, rank your ten items in priority order from 1 (highest priority) to 10 (lowest priority) by writing these numbers in the "Ranking" column. You will have five minutes to complete your rankings. Leave the scoring section blank until the facilitator gives you the instructions.

Your Decision				Scoring (Wait for Instructions)	
Selections	*Ranking*			*Expert Ranking*	*Difference**
_____	_____	**a**	High-speed connection to the Internet for all team members	_____	_____
_____	_____	**b**	A superb search engine	_____	_____
_____	_____	**c**	E-mail	_____	_____
_____	_____	**d**	Threaded text discussion	_____	_____
_____	_____	**e**	Instant messenger (IM) software	_____	_____
_____	_____	**f**	Online meeting capability that includes whiteboard, application sharing, and chat features	_____	_____
_____	_____	**g**	Video teleconference capability	_____	_____
_____	_____	**h**	Web portals that allow shared folders, e-mail exchanges, and collaboration on documents both synchronously and asynchronously	_____	_____
_____	_____	**i**	The industry's ranking of the top ten collaborative tools currently available	_____	_____
_____	_____	**j**	Hyperlinks to the websites of Fortune 100 leading practitioners in virtual teaming	_____	_____
_____	_____	**k**	List of best practices in telecommuting	_____	_____
_____	_____	**l**	Names and e-mail addresses of "virtual team veterans" in your own organization	_____	_____

Selections	*Ranking*		*Expert Ranking*	*Difference**
_____	_____	**m** A list of ten lessons learned by successful virtual teams	_____	_____
_____	_____	**n** Names and e-mail addresses of five people outside your organization who are well-versed in virtual collaboration and who have strong team skills	_____	_____
_____	_____	**o** A strong basis for trust and respect among potential team members across cultures	_____	_____
_____	_____	**p** Names of knowledgeable e-commerce professionals	_____	_____
_____	_____	**q** Expertise in developing and delivering web-based presentations	_____	_____
_____	_____	**r** Shared performance expectations and standards for virtual team work	_____	_____
_____	_____	**s** Shared understanding of collaborative virtual work practices	_____	_____
_____	_____	**t** Knowledge of CyberSpec's past projects and current business focus	_____	_____

Total Score = _____

Average Individual Score for Your Group = _____

*Record the difference between your rank and expert rank as a positive number. If only one of you has ranked an item, record the difference between the rank and 11. If neither of you has ranked an item, record a "0."

GLOSSARY OF TERMS

Application sharing   When two or more people are able to simultaneously look at, comment on, and change a document, graphic, or spreadsheet that one of them has created.

Asynchronous   Communication and collaboration that takes place at different times. Examples include e-mail and threaded text discussions.

Chat   Real-time communication between two computer users. Once a chat has been initiated, either user enters text, which will simultaneously appear on the other user's monitor.

Collaboration tools   Any software that makes it easy to communicate and to co-create work products with distant colleagues using the Internet.

E-commerce   When companies develop and deliver goods and services between businesses or between businesses and customers using the Internet.

E-mail   Electronic mail, a system that allows text messages to be sent from one user to another using a network. An e-mail message can also be directed to a number of addresses at once and can provide a way to transmit extra "attached" documents or graphics.

High-speed connectivity   Bandwidth measures the maximum amount of data that can travel an Internet path in a given time. Today, a cable modem is considered high-speed.

Hyperlinks   The ability to "jump" from one part of a document to another or from one media (such as e-mail) to another (such as a website) by the use of "hot spot" text or images. Hyperlinks enable rapid navigation around cyberspace.

Instant messaging (IM)   Background personal computing software where online "buddies" are defined and monitored. All IM systems show a list of who is currently logged into the same IM system. Users select other users with whom to have private, real-time, text-based, or audio conversations.

Interactive online conference	Internet conferencing software that allows participants to ask questions, vote, interact, and chat with the conference host and other participants. This is a step up in sophistication from online presentations in online auditorium space, where participants are passive recipients of information.
Search engines	Websites that aid in the search for information and resources available through the Internet.
Synchronous	Any means of communicating and collaborating that take place simultaneously or in real time. This includes face-to-face meetings, teleconferences, video conferences, and online conferences.
Telecommuting	The practice of connecting to one's workplace using telephones and computers. It usually implies that people spend part of their work week in a physical office with others and part of their work week interacting with others electronically.
Threaded text discussion	Online dialog comments posted to a common space by different people at different times. They are organized by threads under which other comments are indented to allow users to see how the discussion topic evolved.
Video teleconference	A conference in which two of more people can see and hear one another using video signals and audio devices. Video teleconferences require high bandwidth and, until very recently, required an expensive technical infrastructure.
Virtual teams	Teams of people who primarily interact electronically and who may meet face-to-face occasionally.
Web portal	A website that offers a broad array of services such as threaded dialog forums, chat, search engines, and internal or external news. Web portals allow both synchronous and asynchronous interaction among virtual team members. They allow team members to share documents, folders, discussion, and schedules and to collaborate on shared materials.
Whiteboard	Software that allows two or more people to view and electronically draw pictures using the Internet. The resulting images can then be saved or printed by participants.

GUIDELINES FOR REACHING CONSENSUS

Enter into the group task with a commitment to arrive at the best possible solution. Shoulder your share of the responsibility for the group's success, and discuss the task and process openly and candidly. Use flexible patterns of communication so that all members of your group will be able to participate equally and will feel free to speak up when they have a need to do so. Minority opinions should be encouraged; not only will this increase participation, but it could supply information or logic that previously was missing.

The following guidelines will help during the decision-making process:

1. *Think through your own ideas* as well as you can before meeting with the group (but realize that others may know information that you do not).

2. *Express your own opinions and explain yourself fully,* so that the rest of the group has the benefit of all members' thinking.

3. *Listen to the opinions and feelings of all other group members* and be ready to modify your own position on the basis of logic and understanding.

4. *Avoid arguing for your own position* in order to "win" as an individual:, what is "right" is the best collective judgment of the group as a whole.

5. *View disagreements or conflict as helping to clarify the issue* rather than as hindering the process. Do not "give in" if you have serious reservations about an issue; instead, work toward resolution.

6. *Recognize that tension-reducing behavior, such as laughing or kidding, can be useful,* as long as meaningful conflict is not smoothed over prematurely.

7. *Refrain from conflict-reducing techniques* such as voting, averaging, trading, compromising, or giving in to keep the peace.

8. *Monitor interactions among people* as the group attempts to complete its work, and initiate discussions of what is really going on.

9. *Do not assume that an answer is correct* just because there is agreement initially. Discuss the reasons for the answer and explore all possibilities.

GROUP'S TASK

This task is similar to the task you performed individually, but it will be shared by your whole group. Assume that your group comprises the colleagues with whom you must jointly decide the necessary resources for your virtual team. This task will be an exercise in group decision making, and your group will employ the group-consensus method to reach its decision. This means that the final ranking given to each item must be agreed on by *every* member of the group. In many cases, a consensus is difficult to reach. Therefore, not every ranking may meet with everyone's *complete* approval, but each number assigned must be one that every member is willing to accept. You will have approximately 25 minutes for the group task. Remember that "1" indicates the most important item and "10" indicates the least-important item. Leave the scoring section blank until the facilitator gives you scoring instructions.

Group's Decision				Scoring (Wait for Instructions)	
Selections	Ranking			Expert Ranking	Difference*
————	————	**a**	High-speed connection to the Internet for all team members	————	————
————	————	**b**	A superb search engine	————	————
————	————	**c**	E-mail	————	————
————	————	**d**	Threaded text discussion	————	————
————	————	**e**	Instant messenger (IM) software	————	————
————	————	**f**	Online meeting capability that includes whiteboard, application sharing, and chat features	————	————
————	————	**g**	Video teleconference capability	————	————
————	————	**h**	Web portals that allow shared folders, e-mail exchanges, and collaboration on documents both synchronously and asynchronously	————	————
————	————	**i**	The industry's ranking of the top ten collaborative tools currently available	————	————
————	————	**j**	Hyperlinks to the websites of Fortune 100 leading practitioners in virtual teaming	————	————
————	————	**k**	List of best practices in telecommuting	————	————
————	————	**l**	Names and e-mail addresses of "virtual team veterans" in your own organization	————	————

Group's Decision				Scoring (Wait for Instructions)	
Selections	Ranking			Expert Ranking	Difference*
_____	_____	**m**	A list of ten lessons learned by successful virtual teams	_____	_____
_____	_____	**n**	Names and e-mail addresses of five people outside your organization who are well-versed in virtual collaboration and who have strong team skills	_____	_____
_____	_____	**o**	A strong basis for trust and respect among potential team members across cultures	_____	_____
_____	_____	**p**	Names of knowledgeable e-commerce professionals	_____	_____
_____	_____	**q**	Expertise in developing and delivering web-based presentations	_____	_____
_____	_____	**r**	Shared performance expectations and standards for virtual team work	_____	_____
_____	_____	**s**	Shared understanding of collaborative virtual work practices	_____	_____
_____	_____	**t**	Knowledge of CyberSpec's past projects and current business focus	_____	_____

Total Score = _____

Average Individual Score for Your Group = _____

*Record the difference between your rank and expert rank as a positive number. If only one of you has ranked an item, record the difference between the rank and 11. If neither of you has ranked an item, record a "0."

The Experts' Choices and Rationale

Most people say that *Lost in Cyberspace* challenges their assumptions about the key ingredients of effective virtual collaboration. It is very easy to become carried away with the tangible (and exciting) capabilities of new technology while losing sight of the fact that it is people (and their relationships with one another) that determine whether those exciting capabilities will actually be used.

As more and more companies are drawn (or forced) into the virtual environment in order to compete effectively, they will discover that attention to *purpose, people,* and *practices* remain key determinants of collaborative success.

All items are listed in their original order, with a brief rationale after each for the experts' opinions. The top ten items are then repeated in summary form in order by experts' ranking.

a   **High-speed connection to the Internet for all team members**   **ranked 9th**

> A high-speed connection between team members is useful, but only insofar as they also have the collaborative software needed to make the ultimate presentation to CyberSpec. This is one element of technical compatibility that will affect how well and how smoothly the team is able to interact. For most collaborative applications, you don't need a particularly high speed Internet connection, but when time is short and the pressure is on, every minute can count.

b   **A superb search engine**   **not ranked**

> And what is it you plan to be searching for? The task as set out by CyberSpec in the scenario is to demonstrate mastery of virtual collaboration techniques, not to locate resources via the Internet. This ability is largely irrelevant to the task at hand.

c   **E-mail**   **ranked 10th**

> Every team needs at least one asynchronous communication tool that pushes information out to team members in order to overcome the barriers of operating between different time zones. E-mail alone will not enable the team to produce nor to deliver the CyberSpec presentation as specified in the requirements, but it can help the team work around the clock. Long term, the team will need to develop protocols for how they use this tool in order to avoid "info-glut."

d   Threaded text discussion   **not ranked**

Threaded text discussion is the most obvious (and in some ways
most utilitarian) asynchronous tool available. In this particular
case, however, it could slow the team down because it is a "pull"
technology. People must go to the discussion space to see what
others are discussing (pull it down), whereas e-mail communications are "pushed" to their electronic in-box. Unless the threaded
discussion has hyperlinks to a shared library of materials, the
team would be better off using e-mail attachments to route their
work around asynchronously. Also, there is little time for debate
in this scenario. Most decisions are apt to take place in online
meetings where an immediate change can be made.

e   Instant messenger (IM) software   **not ranked**

Although it can be a wonderful tool for strengthening the infor-
mal social bonds within a team, the ability to see who is online
and to chat briefly with them is not—in the short term—critical to
the CyberSpec team. This team will need to have the full synchronous functionality of online meeting software to perform the
range of collaborative tasks involved in this project.

f   Online meeting capability that includes whiteboard,   **ranked 4th**
**   application sharing, and chat features**

The ability of the team to meet synchronously (in real time) via
the Internet to develop presentation materials is absolutely critical. This is the basis of the team's ability to fulfill CyberSpec's
requirement to demonstrate online collaborative capability.
Without the ability to share applications, it is unlikely the team
will have a sufficiently compatible toolkit to prepare CyberSpec's
presentation. A variety of online conferencing tools could meet
this need. Short-term, good facilitation skills in leading online
meetings will be crucial.

| g | **Video teleconference capability** | **not ranked** |

A nice-to-have capability, videoconferencing is unlikely to be available to a newly formed virtual team with no common organizational infrastructure. Video teleconferencing requires significant bandwidth. For remote virtual team members connecting via dial-up modems, it provides no significant advantage in terms of meeting briefing requirements as specified by CyberSpec. Online meeting and web-based presentation technologies are far more important to the success of the team.

| h | **Web portals that allow shared folders, e-mail exchanges, and collaboration on documents both synchronously and asynchronously** | **ranked 7th** |

The team will need a fixed place in cyberspace in which to store, discuss, and edit electronic documents, presentation materials, and examples. Members will need a place to "meet" online, as well as to swap ideas and experiences as they pertain to the CyberSpec project. A web portal fills the technical requirements for virtual collaboration by combining aspects of real-time interaction (such as online meetings) and asynchronous interaction (such as e-mail or threaded discussions). The ability to effectively use a web portal demonstrates the degree of virtual team skill proficiency that CyberSpec is looking for in its potential partners. Users would need not only to know how to use the tools, but to have developed the team protocols that underpin virtual collaboration.

| i | **The industry's ranking of the top ten collaboration tools currently available** | **not ranked** |

Obtaining a ranking of available tools misses the point. The effectiveness of a tool depends on the match between the work that needs to be done and the function of that particular tool, user familiarity, and the collaborative experience of users. Too often we believe that, if we just find the "right" tool, all will be well. This ignores the impact of people's communication and collaboration habits and the need to adapt tools to work processes.

j   **Hyperlinks to the websites of Fortune 100 leading**   **not ranked**
      practitioners in virtual teaming

The ability to reference skilled virtual team practitioners could
conceivably bolster one's credibility with CyberSpec. One could
refer to the experience of these companies as confirmation of
what has been learned about virtual teaming. What CyberSpec is
looking for, however, is the ability to demonstrate virtual team
collaboration, rather than the ability to research what others
have done. They are looking for a mastery of practice, rather
than theory.

k   **List of best practices in telecommuting**   **not ranked**

Telecommuting is a subset of virtual teamwork that tends to focus
on the policy issues of allowing people to work outside a shared
physical location. This has relatively little to do with the problem
at hand. The ability to connect electronically with a remote office
is only a small part of the picture. The central issue is whether
the team has strong virtual collaboration skills and knowledge of
how to make best use of web-based collaboration tools in order
to meet CyberSpec's expectations.

l   **Names and e-mail addresses for "virtual team veterans"**   **ranked 3rd**
      in your own organization

As the project is defined, the ability to demonstrate web-based
collaboration techniques is central. With this in mind, the first
order of business would be to assemble a team that has already
internalized the principles and practices needed to work very
rapidly via the Internet with people they may not have met.
Incorporating virtual team veterans into a group will demonstrate
practical experience in virtual teaming.

m   **A list of ten lessons learned by successful virtual teams**   **not ranked**

These lessons might be nice to have, but virtual team veterans
would already know what does and does not work in collaborating
with people at a distance. Actual experience in time-compressed
web-based collaboration is more useful than general principles.

n **Names and e-mail addresses of five people outside your organization who are well-versed in virtual collaboration and who have strong team skills** ranked 2nd

Bingo! This is the core of the CyberSpec challenge—identifying and linking geographically and organizationally dispersed people who know how to work together without the luxury of face-to-face contact. Strong team skills implies that these people will need far less time than novice team members to define their purpose, set their priorities, assign roles, negotiate collaborative practices, and agree on the fastest and most effective way to do the job. Virtual team skills are as important as familiarity with the technology itself.

o **A strong basis for trust and respect among potential team members across cultures** ranked 1st

Virtual collaboration requires more than simple knowledge of technology or skill in working with others at a distance. Even in short-lived, ad hoc teams like this one, a fundamental requirement of productive collaboration is that all team members have a clear view of "What's in this for me?" and "What's in this for others?" and to what extent they can rely on their teammates to come through as promised. The basis for trust is built by defining what team members expect from one another and by establishing mutual accountability. Establishing the basis for trust and respect across cultural boundaries is one of the first tasks that any virtual team must address. Recent research has defined the concept of "swift" trust that characterizes virtual, short-term groups or teams.

p **Names of knowledgeable e-commerce professionals** not ranked

E-commerce as a field of business endeavor is related to virtual teaming, but does not necessarily require mastery of virtual collaborative practices. Knowing how to display products and services to meet the needs of remote clients via the Internet does not guarantee that one is equally skilled at the collaboration protocols and practices needed to sustain a virtual team. Again, the team would be better off seeking virtual team veterans within its own organization than trying to recruit team members at large.

q **Expertise in developing and delivering web-based presentations** ranked 5th

This is critical. How will you deliver a credible and "highly inter-active web-based presentation" without in-depth knowledge of the range of presentation tools available and of how to use them effectively? This is a crucial element for any virtual team. The knowledge of virtual team skills is the message, but a web-based presentation is the medium. Not everyone has to be experienced in creating and conducting web-based presentations, but some-one has to be!

r **Shared performance expectations and standards for virtual team work** not ranked

While this is a critical issue for long-term teams, a team with only a four-day life cycle is not apt to be in need of these. This is an aspect of team maintenance that helps assure mutual accountability among dispersed virtual co-workers and counter-acts the tendency for team members to "lose touch" with their colleagues.

s **Shared understanding of collaborative virtual work practices** ranked 6th

If a team lacks an understanding of collaborative virtual work practices, it is doubtful that it will be able to meet either the CyberSpec deadline or the expectation that they demonstrate "mastery of synchronous and asynchronous collaborative tools." The team needs to be able to articulate its practices as part of the sales pitch to CyberSpec. Collaborative virtual work practices include the abilities to generate and refine ideas, to organize and integrate work, to sustain team esprit, and to manage boundaries between people effectively—all via technology.

t   **Knowledge of CyberSpec's past projects and current**   **ranked 8th**
business focus

This is important information without which it is unlikely that a team will succeed in its presentation. Starting with the CyberSpec website, the team must determine: Who does CyberSpec have as their current solution provider partners? What business is it in? On what market does it focus? What is its track record? and Who are its clients? This information will help the team frame its presentation to meet CyberSpec's business needs, in addition to demonstrating its web-based collaborative skills.

SUMMARY OF TOP TEN EXPERT RANKINGS

o   A strong basis for trust and respect among potential team members across cultures.

n   Names and e-mail addresses of five people outside your organization who are well-versed in virtual collaboration and who have strong team skills.

l   Names and e-mail addresses for "virtual team veterans" in your own organization.

f   Online meeting capability that includes whiteboard, application sharing, and chat features.

q   Expertise in developing and delivering web-based presentations.

s   Shared understanding of collaborative virtual work practices.

h   Web portals that allow shared folders, e-mail exchanges, and collaboration on documents both synchronously and asynchronously.

t   Knowledge of CyberSpec's past projects and current business focus.

a   High-speed connection to the Internet for all team members.

c   E-mail.

EXPERT PANEL

The authors gratefully acknowledge the experiences, thoughtful suggestions, and insights of the following expert panel, without whom *Lost in Cyberspace* would lack its real-world foundation.

Tita Theodora Beal	CompetitivEdge Learning
Patricia Browning	Buckman Laboratories, Inc.
Robert H. Buckman	Tioga, Inc.
Bernie DeKoven	CoWorking, Inc.
Michael Feldstein	Michael Feldstein & Associates
Jim Fitzhenry	Buckman Laboratories, Inc.
Jenny Gent	Management Centre Europe
Gil Gordon	TeleWork Associates
Dr. Reuben Harris	Naval Postgraduate School
Barry Howard	QED Consulting
Michael Howland	Applied Knowledge Group, Inc.
Julian Lowenthal	The Practec Group
Monica McGrath	Wharton School of Business
Jonathan Powell	LearningBridge
Eileen Sheriden	The Web of Culture
George Simons	Diversophy.com
Jeffrey Stamps	NetAge, Inc.
Steven Sugar	The Game Group
Jim Tebbe	Shell Oil Corporation
Chip Westbrook	Buckman Laboratories, Inc.

RESOURCES

Coutu, D.L. (1998, June). Trust in virtual teams. *Harvard Business Review,* pp. 20–21.

Duarte, D.L., & Snyder, N.T. (1999). *Mastering virtual teams.* San Francisco: Jossey-Bass.

Grenier, R., & Metes, G. (1995). *Going virtual.* Upper Saddle River, NJ: Prentice Hall.

Harvey, D. (2001, March). The inevitability of the collaborative enterprise. *Across the Board.*

Lipnack, J., & Stamps, J. (1993). *The team net factor.* Essex Junction, VT: Oliver Wright.

Meyerson, D., Weick, K.E., & Kramer, R.M. (1996). Swift trust and temporary teams. In R.M. Kramer & T.R. Tyler (Eds.), *Trust in organizations.* Thousand Oaks, CA: Sage.

About the Authors

Alan Richter is the founder and president of QED Consulting. He has consulted to corporations for many years in multiple capacities. Primarily, he has provided strategic consulting services in the human resource development and change management arenas and has designed and developed innovative curricula for corporations and organizations. Dr. Richter has led teams in the development of leadership programs and processes for new managers through senior executives.

He has also designed pioneering instructional products in the areas of leadership, business ethics, workforce diversity, globalization, marketing, technology, and corporate communications. He is the creator of *The Diversity Game*©, an award winning training tool, *The Global Diversity Game*©, and *The Change Cycle Game*™. He has worked closely with many organizations, including American Express, Avon, BellSouth, Chubb, GE, Home Depot, MetLife, NASA, Nokia, Principal Financial Group, PricewaterhouseCoopers, Prudential, Sony, UBSW, the United Nations, and the Wharton School, and has been a presenter at many conferences nationally and internationally.

Carol Willett is executive vice president for learning and innovation at the Applied Knowledge Group, Inc., helping globally dispersed organizations enhance their virtual collaboration skills. Most recently published in *Knowledge Management: Classic and Contemporary Works* (MIT Press, 2000), Willett is the author of numerous articles, team-building tools, and experiential programs that focus on collaboration as it takes place in the virtual world.

As a senior government training executive, she has led development of distance learning and web-based learning solutions for globally dispersed teams in the intelligence community. As an adjunct faculty member of the University of Virginia, she has taught programs ranging from cross-cultural communications and managing organizational change to leadership, decision making, and ethics. She is a frequent presenter at national and international conferences on sustaining virtual work relationships and mastering technology-based collaborative skills.